MATT CHRISTOPHER®

On the Mound with...

MATT CHRISTOPHER®

On the Mound with...
Curt Schilling

Text by Glenn Stout

LITTLE, BROWN AND COMPANY
New York ✥ Boston

Little, Brown and Company

Time Warner Book Group
1271 Avenue of the Americas, New York, NY 10020
Visit our Web site at www.lb-kids.com

First Edition

Matt Christopher ® is a registered trademark of Matt Christopher
Royalties, Inc.

Cover photograph by Chuck Solomon / Sports Illustrated
© Time Inc.

Library of Congress Cataloging-in-Publication Data

Christopher, Matt.
    On the mound with — Curt Schilling / text by Glenn Stout — 1st ed.
        p. cm.
    Summary: A biography of Curt Schilling, star pitcher with the
Arizona Diamondbacks.
    ISBN: 0-316-60736-3
    1. Schilling, Curt — Juvenile literature.   2. Baseball players —
United States — Biography — Juvenile literature.   [1. Schilling, Curt.
2. Baseball players.]   I. Title.

GV865.S353C57 2004
796.357'092 — dc22
[B]   2003052095

10 9 8 7 6 5 4 3

COM-MO

Printed in the United States of America

Contents

Chapter One:

1966–1984

Growing Up with the Game

Of the thousands of baseball players who have appeared in the major leagues, only eight have been born in the state of Alaska. Those are pretty long odds.

But Alaskan-born pitcher Curt Schilling has made a career of beating the odds. After becoming a professional baseball player it took Curt several years before he made it to the major leagues. Then it took several more years before he reached the major leagues to stay. The Red Sox, Orioles, and Astros all gave up on him before he finally proved he had what it took with the Philadelphia Phillies.

The problem wasn't Curt's arm. It was his head. Throughout his first few years in professional baseball, most baseball people expected more from Schilling. He had all the natural ability in the world, but he lacked the discipline to make use of it. He expected baseball to be easy and didn't take the game very seriously. He just didn't realize how hard he had to work in order to succeed.

It wasn't until Curt Schilling learned to commit to doing more that he finally began to succeed as a major league pitcher. Even then the going wasn't easy. Throughout his career he was plagued by a number of injuries and personal tragedies. Yet in the end he made himself not only one of the best pitchers in baseball, but one of the best people in the game, a player who gives his time and energy to help others.

His unlikely story began in Alaska, where his father Cliff, a career soldier, was stationed. On November 14, 1966, Cliff's wife Mary gave birth to a son, Curtis Montague Schilling.

Cliff was a baseball lover who, Curt says, "put a ball and glove in my crib." Baseball was a tough sport to play in Alaska. Had his father remained stationed there, it's possible Curt would not have become a ballplayer. Fortunately Cliff was soon transferred out of Alaska to the lower forty-eight states where the weather made it easier to play baseball.

Curt was what some people call an "army brat," growing up on Army bases and moving every few years when his father was transferred. But no matter where the Schillings lived, Curt loved playing baseball. There are always plenty of children around an Army base and he always had someone to play with.

For as long as he can remember, Curt played baseball. And for as long as he has played baseball, he has been able to throw the ball fast. "It's a natural thing," he once told a sportswriter, "something you are born with." Even when Curt was very young, people noticed how hard he threw. When he was eight years old his father told him, "You have an arm that will let you be what you want to be." Curt's dad was right, but it would take Curt many years to fulfill his father's prophecy.

The Schillings eventually settled off-base in Paradise Valley near Scottsdale, Arizona. Curt loved the sunny Arizona weather. Nearly every day was perfect for playing baseball.

Curt played in local youth leagues. But he wasn't a pitcher. With his strong arm he played third base. He was one of the few players who could throw the ball accurately all the way across the diamond from third base to first.

Curt was still a third baseman when he started to attend Shadow Mountain High School. He was beginning to realize that he threw harder than most other high school players. When he was in his junior year the Cincinnati Reds held a tryout camp near his home town. Curt decided to attend.

He was just one of more than a hundred young players hoping to grab the attention of the Reds scouts. Even though major league teams scour the country looking for prospects, they still hold occasional open tryout camps to make sure they don't miss any good young players. At seventeen years old, Curt was one of the youngest players at the tryout. Many of the other players were young men from local colleges. Curt knew if he was going to get the scouts to notice him, he'd have to show them something spectacular.

Before the tryouts, the scouts took every player's name and attached a number to his back. The players were then lined up to participate in drills. Traditionally, the first drill is a timed dash, usually 40 yards. For many players, the timed run is the closest they come to the major leagues. Unless they run it quickly enough they aren't considered prospects and are sent home.

Pitchers, however, are excluded from the run. Scouts don't care if they can run fast or not. They only care how fast they can throw. Curt knew he couldn't run very well and was afraid he'd miss the cut before he got a chance to hit or do anything else. He had done some pitching, so he got in line with the other pitchers.

After warming up, each player was sent to the pitchers' mound to throw to a catcher. One scout stood near the mound with a notebook, taking down the pitcher's number and calling it out so the other scouts knew who was throwing. One scout stood behind the backstop with a radar gun to measure how fast each pitcher threw.

Most high school pitchers throw about 75 miles per hour. Even though few people can consistently hit a baseball thrown that hard, 75 miles per hour isn't nearly fast enough to succeed as a professional pitcher. College pitchers typically throw at least 80 miles per hour and professional pitchers throw at least 85 miles per hour. Some, like Randy Johnson and Curt Schilling, can throw 100 miles per hour.

Curt didn't throw that hard — yet. But he did throw hard.

When the scout called his name Curt stood on the mound and placed his toe on the rubber. He had pitched a little, so he was confident he could throw the ball over the plate. But he had no idea how hard he threw.

He took a deep breath and then started a slow windup, lifting his arms over his head, turning his body and then stepping toward home plate while throwing the ball with all his might. *Pop!* The ball slammed into the catcher's mitt and the sound echoed across the diamond. Other players turned their heads when they heard it and started to watch.

The scout behind the plate looked at the number on the radar gun and wrote it down. The catcher threw the ball back to Curt. He wound up and threw again.

Pop! Once again the ball rifled into the catcher's mitt. The scene was repeated another ten or twelve times before the scout told Curt that was enough. As Curt stepped away from the mound, another scout at the camp approached him and asked his name. Then he said something that startled Curt.

"You hit ninety miles per hour on the gun," he said. Curt couldn't believe it. He knew he threw hard, but he didn't know he could throw *that* hard.

The scout then started asking Curt all sorts of questions, like where he went to school and the name of his coach. Then he asked if he was a senior.

"I'm just a junior," said Curt.

The scout shook his head. The Reds were looking for players they could sign to a professional contract in the next draft. To be eligible to play professionally, young men had to be eighteen years old or be a high school graduate. As a high school junior, Curt wouldn't be eligible to be drafted for another year. The scout sent him away, but told him the Reds wouldn't forget about him. In the meantime he told Curt to keep pitching.

From that moment on, Curt knew he was a pitcher. As he said later, "I knew I was too slow to run the bases."

Although he still made occasional appearances in the field, in his senior year Curt focused on pitching. That was fine with Curt's coach. The Shadow

7

Mountain Mustangs were one of the most success-ful baseball programs in the Phoenix area and he could always use another pitcher.

The Mustangs already had a deep and experi-enced pitching staff, led by seniors Rick Rock, David Cassidy, and Ed Janashak. They all deserved to pitch and the Shadow Mountain coach made sure that everyone got a chance. Although Curt did well, he didn't have the opportunity to pitch as much as he would have liked.

But Curt did more than just play baseball in high school. One of his friends had one of the first Apple home computers. Curt took one look at the com-puter and was hooked. He soon had his own and has since described himself as a "geek."

Curt was a good student in most subjects. But when he was really interested in the subject, he was outstanding. Then he had to learn everything he possibly could about it, and sometimes neglected his work in other subjects. He particularly enjoyed history.

But baseball was still the most important thing in Curt's life. He believed he had the talent and drive to make it as a professional ballplayer. In order to do that, he knew it would be best if he attended college. Although major league teams were expressing interest in Curt, he hadn't been pitching very long and was still unpolished. He wasn't considered a sure-fire prospect and was likely to be drafted in the lower rounds. Players drafted in the lower rounds don't receive a great deal of money — or a lot of time to prove themselves. He knew he could end up just playing a year and then getting released. And once he signed a professional contract, he wouldn't be eligible to play in college.

Playing baseball in college made the most sense, but Curt wasn't receiving scholarship offers from the schools he wanted to go to. But Yavapai Junior College, a community college in nearby Prescott, Arizona, had a terrific baseball program. Many students attend junior college for a year or two, adjusting to college life and improving their skills before transferring to a four-year school. Curt decided to play in a summer league, then attend Yavapai in the fall of 1985 and play baseball for the school the following spring. If he had a good year for Yavapai, he knew that a four-year school might offer him a scholarship. If he had a great year, he knew that he might even be drafted in the next pro baseball draft. After all, he was still growing, still improving, and still learning to pitch. An additional year of experience was certain to help.

Curt worked hard during the summer baseball season and improved his pitching. When he entered Yavapai in the fall, coach David Dangler already expected him to be a key pitcher in the upcoming season. Dangler was one of the most successful junior college coaches in the country and his Yavapai Roughriders were usually a powerhouse. The team played in one of the best junior college leagues, the Arizona Community College Athletic Conference. Scouts from the major leagues and other colleges flocked to their games. Each year, four-year colleges recruited many players from the league and a couple of players from every team were usually drafted by the major leagues. Curt would have a great opportunity to show what he could do. If he succeeded, he was certain to be noticed.

He didn't know it yet, but some major league teams were already very interested in him. Ever since he had shown up at the Reds' tryout camp, local pro scouts had tracked his progress. At the time, there were two drafts each year for amateur players, one in June and the other in January. The June draft was by far the most important, because it was then that each major league team selected dozens and dozens of players from the pool of draftees. In fact, the June draft so overshadowed the January one that the January one was being phased out. It would be held for the last time in 1986.

Boston Red Sox scout Ray Boone, a former major league player, noticed how rapidly Curt was improving. Curt reminded Boone of his contemporary, Hall of Fame pitcher Robin Roberts, known for his fastball, his stamina, and his toughness. Boone thought Schilling might someday become the same kind of pitcher. Curt's blazing fastball and surprising control marked him as a hot prospect. The scouts liked his size, too. Curt was tall, strong, and broad-shouldered, the perfect build for a pitcher. He stood almost six foot four and weighed over 200 pounds. Most scouts believe that tall, stocky pitchers like Curt put less strain on their arms and are less likely to get hurt than smaller, skinnier pitchers.

Boone convinced the Red Sox to make Schilling their second round pick in the 1986 January draft.

On draft day, Curt waited by the phone. It finally rang and he discovered that he had been drafted by the Boston Red Sox in the second round.

The pick was what is known as a "draft and follow." The Red Sox would have up to a year to offer Curt a contract. They planned to watch him closely in junior college and then decide whether or not to sign him.

Although Curt was disappointed not to be drafted in the first round or to receive a contract right away, he was thrilled to be drafted by the Red Sox. The team had experienced several poor seasons in a row. Curt hoped that meant there would be an opportunity for him to make the major leagues quickly.

All he had to do was prove that he was the man for the job. Curt Schilling was determined to do just that.

Chapter Two:
1984-1985

Going to School

When the Yavapai baseball team began practice that winter, Curt quickly discovered that he still had a great deal to learn about pitching. In high school Curt had just thrown his fastball right down the middle of the plate. Few high school batters had been able to hit his pitches.

College hitters were much better. Even when pitching against his own teammates during scrimmage games, he was hit hard. Every hitter in college was at least as good as the best hitters in high school. Most of them could hit his fastball. He quickly realized that if he was going to succeed in college baseball he would have to bear down on the field just like he did in the classroom. He would have to do more than just throw. He had to learn how to pitch, to throw his fastball to spots, change speeds, and throw his curveball for a strike.

His coaches worked with Curt on his windup to help him with his control. Unless a pitcher uses the same windup on every pitch it is almost impossible to throw strikes. At first, Curt's arms and legs flew all over the place. The coaches taught him to slow down and stay balanced. When the regular season started Curt could hardly wait to get on the mound.

Yavapai opened the season in a tournament and dropped their first two games. Curt took the mound for the third game. He was determined to win.

The team from Pima Community College was tough. But Curt hit his spots and mixed his pitches well. Although he was in and out of trouble for much of the game, he won, 6–4.

Curt quickly became the most dependable pitcher on the Yavapai staff. Although coach Dangler usually started Schilling on the mound, he wasn't afraid to use Curt in relief, either. Curt seemed to thrive on the work.

Red Sox scouts watched him in almost every appearance. Even though he was sometimes being hit hard and occasionally struggled with control, his improvement was obvious. Ever so slowly he was learning to harness his natural ability to throw hard. The scouts knew they had to take into consideration the fact that Curt was facing hitters who used aluminum bats. Aluminum springs back into shape when struck; wood doesn't. So when a ball hits an aluminum bat, it is catapulted farther than when it hits a wooden bat. Therefore, the metal bats make it possible to get hits even when the ball isn't struck with the fat part of the bat.

Professional baseball uses only wooden bats. The scouts believed that when Curt pitched against hitters using wooden bats, he would be much more successful. Pitches that were now hits would become easy outs.

But the scouts were even more impressed by Curt's attitude and effort. He pitched aggressively and wasn't afraid of throwing strikes. And late in the game, when most pitchers tired, Curt seemed to get a second wind. He also appeared to put the team first. He didn't mind giving up runs as long as his team won.

And Yavapai did a lot of winning. For the season they averaged almost ten runs per game. Curt took advantage of all the run support he received and won almost every time he pitched.

Yavapai finished league play in first place in their division with a record of 17–9. Curt won ten games and lost only twice. But in the league tournament, the long season finally caught up with Curt. In two appearances he gave up a lot of runs, although he went 1–1. Nevertheless, Yavapai still won the league championship. They then went on to finish a surprising third in the Junior College World Series.

For the season, Yavapai finished 37–17. Curt led the team with 11 wins and 3 losses. He also led the team with 71 strikeouts in 102 innings. But his earned run average, a statistic that measures how many runs a pitcher gives up for every nine innings pitched, was 7.54 — one of the highest ERAs on the team. Still, the pro scouts were all pleased with his progress. They were far more concerned with what they saw with their own eyes, rather than what the statistics said. And what they saw pleased them.

The Red Sox had six more months to decide whether to sign Curt to a contract. Meanwhile, other teams were watching Curt and hoping that he would decide to stay in school. If he did, Boston's right to sign him would expire the following January and he would enter the draft again. Then, any team could draft him.

The Red Sox didn't want that to happen. All season long they told Curt that they would offer him a contract at the end of the season. At the same time, Curt was becoming impatient. He had been looking forward to playing professional baseball his whole life and didn't want to spend another season in school. If he didn't turn professional now, there was always a chance that he would get hurt. The likelihood of the Red Sox signing an injured player was not very good. So when the Sox finally offered him a contract for an undisclosed amount of money, he accepted. On May 30, 1986, college ended for Curt and a career as a professional ballplayer began.

Chapter Three:
1985–1988

Learning in the Pros

Curt Schilling was confident that he was ready to play professional baseball. But he had no idea that the greatest challenge he would face would be off the field. For the first time in his life, Schilling had to learn to live on his own.

After he was drafted, Curt spent time packing and saying goodbye to his family and friends. The Red Sox had ordered him to report to Elmira, New York, home of their single-A minor league affiliate in the New York–Pennsylvania League.

All of a sudden, there would be no one telling him when to go to bed or get up, no one to do his laundry or cook his meals, no one to tell him right and wrong. Schilling's father, with his military background, had always been strict with his son. Now Schilling would make up his own rules.

The Red Sox showed their confidence in Schilling by sending him to Elmira. The minor leagues are organized into three levels — triple-A, double-A, and single-A — and major league teams assign their players to each level according to ability. The best players go to triple-A and the next best go to double-A. The rawest recruits are assigned to single-A. The Red Sox controlled five minor league teams, including three teams in single-A. The youngest and least experienced players usually began their careers with the Winter Haven team of the Florida State League. But the Red Sox believed that Schilling didn't need to start his career at the very bottom. Elmira, in the New York–Pennsylvania League, was for players with more talent and promise.

On the field Schilling adjusted quickly to pro baseball. Just as the scouts had thought, Schilling was much more successful when pitching against batters using wooden bats. His fastball, which now topped 90 miles per hour on the radar gun, overpowered many hitters. Even when they hit the ball, few hit it very hard. As he gained confidence in throwing his fastball, his control improved.

Off the field, however, Schilling began to develop

some bad habits. In between pitching appearances he had a lot of fun. Like many young players living on their own for the first time, Schilling spent his free time partying and goofing off. Some professional players ruin their careers by spending more time having fun than learning to play baseball. Others get into trouble with drugs and alcohol or simply fail to stay in shape. They are simply not mature enough to live on their own.

Even though Schilling was all business on the mound, it was a different story away from the ballpark. At first, Schilling could still stay up all night and pitch well the next day. Eventually, however, his failure to take care of himself would impact his career.

The Red Sox were one of the few major league organizations that didn't supply a full-time pitching coach to their minor league affiliates. Instead, former pitcher Lee Stange served as the club's roving pitching instructor. Every few weeks he spent some time with the Elmira team, working with the pitchers. Then he did the same for another of Boston's minor league teams. Although he did a good job when he was there, in between his visits the pitchers received very little instruction. There were times that Schilling felt a little lost on the mound.

He survived his first minor league season on raw talent, finishing with a record of 7–3 and an impressive 2.59 ERA. He was successful despite the fact that there were times he didn't know what he was doing on the mound. Still, although he didn't make the league All-Star team, at age nineteen he was clearly the best pitcher on the Elmira team and a rising star in the league. Red Sox fans following the minor leagues knew that Schilling was a player to watch.

It was an exciting time to be a member of the Red Sox organization. After the end of the minor league season in early September 1986, Schilling followed the Red Sox as they won the American League Eastern Division and pennant. They then played the New York Mets of the National League for the world championship.

Schilling enjoyed watching the Red Sox in the World Series, particularly star pitcher Roger Clemens. The 1986 season was Clemens's first full season in the major leagues. Although he was only four years older than Schilling, Clemens's record of 24–4 for the season marked him as one of the best pitchers in baseball.

Like Schilling, Clemens was a classic power pitcher, someone who challenged hitters with a fastball. That was precisely the kind of pitcher Schilling wanted to be someday. As he watched the Series he dreamed of joining Clemens on the Boston pitching staff and pitching in the World Series himself.

After five games, the Red Sox needed to win only once more to take the Series. The Red Sox hadn't won the World Series since 1918 and their fans were hungry for a world championship. But in game six, only one out away from victory, the Red Sox collapsed. The Mets won the game and then won game seven two days later to win the Series. The Red Sox and their fans were devastated. In a short time, the fallout from their defeat would have an impact on Curt Schilling's career.

In the spring of 1987 Schilling reported to Boston's spring training camp in Winter Haven, Florida. Although he was assigned to minor league camp, he still had the opportunity to watch the Red Sox major leaguers work out. That made him even more eager and determined to make the major leagues.

His performance during the 1987 season was strong enough to earn him a promotion to the Red Sox best single-A club, Greensboro of the South Atlantic League. He hoped to continue to rise through the Red Sox farm system.

But the 1988 season would be an up-and-down year for Schilling. The Greensboro team wasn't very good and Schilling had difficulty winning. It didn't help that he was trying to learn to pitch without the help of a pitching coach. Although Schilling occasionally picked up tips from the other pitchers, figuring out what worked for him, what didn't, and why, was a process of trial and error.

Most of the time Schilling just tried to strike people out. While he was successful in that goal, leading the league with 189 strikeouts, he finished the year with a record of only 8–15. At the season's end, he began to wonder about his future in baseball.

Schilling spent the winter back in Arizona. His father had been forced to retire from the military after twenty-two years due to heart trouble and had moved to Colorado. Then, after taking a job in law enforcement, Cliff Schilling had been diagnosed with a brain tumor. The prognosis wasn't very good. In January, before he became too ill to travel, he returned to Arizona to visit with his son.

In many ways, it was the first time the father and son had spent time together as adults. Knowing their time together was precious, they spent much of the week talking. Every time Curt expressed doubt that he would ever reach the major leagues, his father kept reassuring him that he would.

The night before his father was scheduled to return to Colorado, he and Curt stayed up almost the entire night. "I know it sounds weird," said Schilling later, "but we stayed up late that night just talking about baseball, life, everything. He said things that a father usually thinks but doesn't say. I remember him saying how he knew I was going to make it to the big leagues."

The next morning they both got up early so Cliff Schilling could catch his plane back to Colorado. Then, as they were preparing to leave the house, Cliff collapsed. He was suffering from an aortic aneurysm, a condition that causes part of the aorta,

24

the artery that connects to the heart, to bulge. Curt held his father in his arms as he called 9-1-1 and waited for the paramedics. They arrived within minutes, but it was too late. Cliff Schilling died in his son's arms. Curt had to tell his mother that her husband was dead.

Schilling was crushed by his father's death. But the last conversation he'd had with Cliff had filled him with determination to make it to the major leagues. His father had believed in him. Curt would honor that belief by trying his best to succeed.

It wasn't easy. Just a few weeks after his father died, Curt had to push everything aside and go to spring training. At the end of camp he was assigned to the club's double-A affiliate in New Britain, Connecticut.

Double-A baseball is a big step up from single-A. Only the very best prospects are promoted to double-A. Some players even go from double-A directly to the major leagues. For many pro players, a season in double-A either makes or breaks their career.

The New Britain Red Sox played at Beehive Field, one of the best pitcher's parks in the minor leagues.

Batters had a hard time hitting home runs there, where it was nearly 500 feet to the fence in center field.

Schilling succeeded in making batters hit fly balls that his outfielders ran down and caught, but his strikeout numbers dropped dramatically. What had worked in single-A didn't work against better competition in double-A. Even though Schilling was 8–5 for the season, he was beginning to become frustrated. Without his father he felt very alone and started to act up more. He listened to heavy metal music and partied hard between every start. His teammates thought he was a lot of fun but they also thought he was a little crazy. Some people in the Red Sox organization were starting to question whether or not he was serious enough about his career to make it to the major leagues.

In midsummer, the Red Sox thought they had a chance to win the pennant and make it back to the World Series. Red Sox fans were still bitter over their loss to the Mets in 1986 and the team felt pressure to do everything it possibly could to win. As Boston general manager Lou Gorman said later,

"We owed it to our fans to try to get back to the Series." When starting pitcher Dennis Boyd started having arm trouble in midseason, the Red Sox decided they needed to acquire another experienced major league pitcher. None of their minor league pitchers, including Schilling, was ready for the majors yet.

The Baltimore Orioles were far out of the pennant race and ready to rebuild with younger players. Starting pitcher Mike Boddiker was a star, but his talents were going to waste with the Orioles. His contract was due to run out at the end of the season and, given Baltimore's performance, the team knew he was unlikely to stay with the Orioles. The Orioles knew that if they offered him in trade before then, they could get some good prospects in return.

The Red Sox called the Orioles and asked if they wanted to trade Boddiker. The Orioles said they did and the two teams started negotiating.

Every major league team is constantly scouting players from other teams so they know whom to ask for in trades. The Orioles were particularly interested in an outfielder named Brady Anderson who was currently playing for Boston's triple-A team. The Red Sox reluctantly agreed to trade Anderson, who they considered their best young player.

But Baltimore also wanted a young pitcher. The two teams discussed several players before the Red Sox finally offered Schilling. At best, Boston thought Schilling was still three or four years away from the major leagues, and people in the organization were starting to whisper about his off-the-field behavior.

But Baltimore had done their homework in regard to Schilling. Unlike the Red Sox, the Orioles spent a great deal of time working with their young pitchers in the minor leagues. They thought that Schilling had been wasting his time in the Boston organization and that some of his off-the-field problems were due to his frustration. With some instruction and direction, they thought he could become a big winner.

The deal was made on July 29. Boddiker joined the Red Sox and Anderson and Schilling became property of the Orioles. Although Boston general manager Lou Gorman later said that they were "really impressed" with Schilling, at the time, the Red Sox hardly gave the loss of Schilling a thought.

At first, Schilling was upset with the trade. The Orioles were awful and would finish the season in last place with a record of 54–107. Schilling didn't really want to play for an organization whose future looked so bleak. When a reporter asked him about the trade, he made his feelings clear.

The Orioles assigned Schilling to their double-A franchise in Charlotte, North Carolina for the rest of the season. Although he had been disgruntled at first, he soon realized that the trade provided him with a great opportunity. Unlike the Red Sox, the Orioles were actually trying to teach him how to pitch. They were desperate for pitching help and Schilling immediately became one of their top prospects. Over the final month of the season he went 5–2.

The minor league season ends at the beginning of September, one month before the end of the major league regular season. Most minor league players look forward to returning home after a long season.

But the Orioles were going nowhere. In September, major league teams are allowed to add as many as fifteen players to their major league roster. Many teams use this to provide a few extra bodies for the pennant race or to take a look at minor leaguers.

Curt Schilling got a call and was told to report to the Orioles. Just like his father had said eight months earlier, he was going to the major leagues.

Chapter Four:
1988–1991

Ups and Downs

The Orioles didn't call Schilling up to the major leagues just so he could sit on the bench. Manager Frank Robinson, a former outfielder and member of the Baseball Hall of Fame, wanted to see Schilling pitch. When the young pitcher joined the team, Robinson told him he would start against his old team, the Boston Red Sox, on September 7.

Schilling was thrilled. He had been looking forward to making the major leagues since he had been a young boy. Now, not only was he in the major leagues, but he was going to start a game against the team that had signed him and then traded him away.

Even though the game didn't matter to the Orioles, it was a big game for the Red Sox. The Sox led the American League East by only two games. They needed to win every game they could.

Schilling could hardly believe he was in the majors playing with players he had watched on television, like Oriole shortstop Cal Ripken. Of course, they could hardly believe that Schilling was pitching for them, either. When Schilling first walked into the locker room they could hardly believe what they were seeing.

Schilling was wearing an earring and had dyed a streak of his hair bright blue. He also had a big tattoo of a rottweiler on his arm. His teammates had heard that he was a little wild, but they weren't quite prepared for what they saw. When he bounced into the clubhouse with a big smile on his face, one of the veterans yelled, "What are you smiling at, bush?" The crack was meant to remind Schilling that he was bush league, still green.

Schilling just laughed. He was nervous and excited but he wasn't intimidated. He couldn't help thinking about his father. So he did something special.

Every big league player can get free tickets to games and they can leave tickets for friends at the ticket office. Schilling left a ticket under his father's name. In every game he has played in since, he has left a ticket in his father's memory. The knowledge that there is an empty seat in the stands for his father helps him stay focused.

Despite the Orioles' poor record, more than 35,000 fans filled Baltimore's Memorial Stadium for the game against the Red Sox. Schilling had never pitched before such a large crowd. In the minors, there were usually only a few thousand people in the stands. His mind was a blur as he warmed up in the bull pen, listened to the national anthem, and then heard the public address announcer call out, "Pitching for the Orioles tonight, Curt Schilling." It was like a dream.

But Schilling knew that if he didn't concentrate on what he was supposed to do, the dream could turn into a nightmare. The Red Sox were one of the best teams in baseball.

He stood on the mound and looked at his catcher, Mickey Tettleton. He took the sign for the first pitch, a fastball. He tried not to notice that the hitter was Boston third baseman, Wade Boggs. In seven major league seasons Boggs had won four batting titles, including the last three. He would soon win another in 1988 with a .366 batting average.

The first hitter Schilling faced was the best hitter

in baseball. What a way to start a major league career! Butterflies fluttered in his stomach as Schilling took a deep breath, wound up and threw. Boggs, well known for his patience, took the pitch.

The butterflies in Schilling's stomach started to disappear. They went away entirely a moment later when Boggs swung and bounced a ground ball to Cal Ripken for an easy out.

The next batter, Marty Barrett, singled. But Schilling stayed calm and retired Dwight Evans and Mike Greenwell to record a scoreless first inning.

In the second, he chalked up his first major league strikeout, sending Todd Benzinger back to the dugout. The Orioles then pushed across a run and Schilling led, 1–0.

Schilling nursed the lead into the fourth inning when Ellis Burks homered to tie the game. Then, in the fifth inning, Schilling hit a batter, gave up a single to Boggs, and walked a hitter to load the bases.

Red Sox outfielder Dwight Evans stepped to the plate. He was known as one of the toughest outs in baseball. He proved his reputation to Schilling. He ripped a double to left field, knocking in two runners. Now Schilling trailed 3–1. Manager Frank

Robinson had a relief pitcher start warming up. Schilling looked like he was just about finished.

But he worked his way out of the inning and managed to pitch a scoreless sixth and seventh. By then, Robinson decided he had pitched enough. He didn't want Schilling to throw too many pitches and hurt his arm. He removed him from the game trailing 3–1.

Even though he was behind, it was an impressive debut for a pitcher only twenty-one years old. It was soon made even better when the Orioles stormed back in the ninth inning to win the game 4–3. Even though Schilling wasn't credited with the win, he knew that he had done his job and kept his team in the game. He hoped he had made the Red Sox regret their decision to trade him.

The Boston players had been impressed and told reporters that Schilling had good stuff. His fastball was fast and moved a little at the last second. He also had a decent curveball.

A week later, this time in Boston, Schilling received another start. But now the Red Sox knew what he had and this time, things didn't go quite so well. In only one and two-thirds innings, he gave up five hits. Boston raced to a 4–0 lead before Schilling was removed from the game, eventually taking the loss in Baltimore's 6–1 defeat.

Still, Schilling was thrilled to be in the big leagues — maybe a little too thrilled. When he received his first major league paycheck, worth just over $5000 for two weeks work, he felt rich. In the minors he had made only a few hundred dollars a month.

He raced to the bank and cashed the check, asking the clerk to give him all $5000 in twenty-dollar bills. Then, afraid he might get robbed, he took a cab back to his hotel. He went to his room, dumped the money on his bed, and rolled around on it, throwing it up in the air and screaming with delight. As Schilling later recalled, "I remember thinking, 'This is more money than I'll spend in my entire life. I've made it. Nothing can stop me now.'"

But over the next few weeks Schilling would learn that success wasn't such a sure thing. In his next two appearances he was shelled and lost both games. His first taste of the big leagues ended with a 0–3 record.

Schilling had made an impression on the Orioles. Unfortunately, it wasn't the kind of impression he wanted to leave. Apart from his first game against the Red Sox, he hadn't played that well. Off the field, he was getting a reputation as a partyer. He spent almost every night out on the town, drinking and having fun. And the longer he stayed in the majors, the wilder he acted.

"I was such a screwup when I got to the big leagues," he later recalled. "I was a total idiot. I ran the nightlife, I drank, I just acted crazy. I did all the stupid things you'd expect from a twenty-one-year-old kid with money. I can't believe what a dope I was."

Neither could the Orioles. Although they still believed he was major league material, it was obvious he had a lot of growing up to do.

Unfortunately, he showed few signs of doing that very fast. After spending most of the 1989 season with the Baltimore triple-A team in Rochester, Schilling returned to the major leagues in September of 1989, but again he struggled. Many people expected him to make the team the following spring, but he didn't pitch very well and was sent down to Rochester again. But the Orioles were desperate for pitching. They recalled him to the big leagues midway through the season.

Schilling bounced into the Baltimore clubhouse as carefree and crazy as he had been two years earlier. He still had the earring and still had his hair dyed blue. He also had his hair cut into a mohawk.

Manager Frank Robinson had seen enough. It was obvious that Schilling wasn't going to grow up on his own. He needed some help. He called Schilling into his office. The pitcher bounced in and flopped into a chair.

As a player, Robinson had been known as one of the toughest guys in the game. As a manager, he had a short fuse but tried to be patient. But Curt Schilling had just about exhausted his patience.

It wasn't that there was anything wrong with the hair or the earring; it was Schilling's attitude that bothered Robinson. Schilling just didn't seem to care about his performance. Whatever happened seemed to be okay with him, and Robinson knew he would never become a consistent winner with that attitude.

The manager just sat there staring at Schilling. With each passing moment, the young pitcher grew more uncomfortable.

Suddenly Robinson said, "What's *wrong* with you, son?"

Schilling was taken aback. "Uh, what do you mean?" he blurted out.

Robinson spelled it out for him; it was time to get serious. "First of all," he said, "you don't throw an inning for me until that earring is gone. Second, I expect you to look and act professional."

Schilling paid attention — sort of. He left Robinson's office, got rid of the earring and cut his hair. Outwardly, he was a changed person, and for the rest of the year, pitching in relief, he was a valuable member of the Orioles pitching staff. "He wasn't a bad kid," recalled Robinson later. "He just wanted to be noticed."

Near the end of the season Schilling met a young woman named Shonda Brewer. Shonda worked for a Baltimore-based cable television station called Home Team Sports. Curt invited the whole crew out to a bar and picked up the tab. A short time later he was at a shopping mall and saw her again. The two started talking and Schilling asked her to dinner. She agreed.

When she told her friends at the station later, they looked at her like she was nuts. Schilling had a reputation for running around and doing crazy things. He'd never had a girlfriend for very long. "Stay away from him," they warned her.

But he met Shonda at the perfect time. He was starting to settle down and she recognized that. Over the next few months they spent more and more time together. Schilling even stayed in Baltimore after the season to be with her. They looked forward to getting to know each other even better in the upcoming season. Since they both worked in Baltimore, they would have ample time.

The Orioles were improving rapidly and were close to challenging for the playoffs. Then general manager Roland Hemond thought he saw an opportunity to help the team. The Houston Astros were rebuilding and looking to trade first baseman Glenn Davis, a valuable slugger. Hemond thought Davis could really help the Orioles.

Manager Frank Robinson agreed. The Astros

wanted prospects in exchange for Davis. Hemond asked Robinson whom he thought the Orioles could spare. "Anybody but Schilling," he said.

But when Hemond started negotiating with the Astros, they kept asking for Schilling. Hemond finally relented in January of 1991, trading Schilling, pitcher Pete Harnisch, and outfielder Steve Finley to the Astros for Davis.

Robinson was angry when he found out. So was Schilling. So was Shonda Brewer. Schilling asked her to follow him to Houston. Although they had only known each other for four months, they had already decided to spend the rest of their lives together. She moved to Houston and the couple was married in 1992.

The Astros had plans for their new pitcher. They wanted Schilling to become their closer. They thought that his fastball and carefree personality made him perfect for the role.

But when Schilling opened the 1991 season in the bull pen, he was absolutely awful. A closer needs to throw strikes and Schilling was walking too many people. He blew save after save and in June was finally sent back to the Astros triple-A team in Tucson.

Schilling couldn't stand being back in the minors. One day he called up Astros pitching coach Bob Cluck on the phone and pleaded with him, "Get me out of here. I want out!"

Cluck turned him down cold. "Let me tell you something," he said. "Up here it doesn't matter if you throw a great fastball down the middle and the guy pops it up or if you make a great pitch and he breaks a bat and gets a hit. It's *all* about results."

Cluck made Schilling start thinking. So far in his career he had always blamed something or someone else for his own failures. He began to realize that he had to take responsibility for what happened when he pitched. It *was* all about results.

He began to pitch better almost immediately and was soon back up with the Astros. But he had lost his place as the team's closer. They didn't believe in him anymore. His career was at a crossroads. But Schilling didn't know it.

Chapter Five:
1992

A Conversation with the Rocket

One January morning in 1992, Schilling made his way to the Astrodome, where the Astros played, to work out. The Astros had a small gym with weights and other exercise equipment so their players could stay in shape during the season and make use of it in the offseason if they were in the area.

Schilling lived nearby and occasionally stopped by to work out. He knew that if he didn't the Astros would be mad at him. So he showed up a couple of times each week, but he didn't work very hard unless a coach was watching him. He figured that he was in good enough shape already. He spent most of his time talking and joking with other players.

Occasionally players from other big league teams in the Houston area would also use the Astros facility. On this particular day, Schilling walked into the room and spotted Roger Clemens, the great Boston pitcher, working out. He often saw Clemens there during the offseason.

Although Clemens was only four years older than Schilling, he had been pitching in the major leagues since 1984 and was recognized as one of the greatest pitchers in baseball. He had won twenty games or more in three different seasons. In one game he even struck out twenty batters, a major league record. At Schilling's age Clemens had already won the first of three Cy Young awards for best pitcher in the American League and appeared in a World Series. The thought of Curt Schilling achieving any of those milestones was laughable.

Like Schilling, Clemens was a power pitcher whose devastating fastball earned him the nickname "The Rocket." In fact, when baseball scouts looked at Schilling, he reminded them of Clemens, with one big difference. Unlike Schilling, Roger Clemens was focused on his career and committed to doing everything he could to stay in shape and get better. His workouts were legendary as he put his body through a series of torturous exercises to prepare for the demands of pitching. When Schilling sauntered

44

into the exercise room that day, Clemens had already been working out for hours. His shirt was soaked with sweat and he was breathing heavily as he hoisted weights.

Schilling and Clemens knew each other slightly from spring training during Schilling's brief career with the Red Sox. Clemens remembered the great game Schilling had thrown against the Red Sox in his major league debut for the Orioles in 1988. But apart from exchanging a nod or a quick hello, the two pitchers had never really spoken before. Schilling thought Clemens was a little stuck up.

He wasn't. But seeing Curt Schilling made him mad, and every time he saw him he got madder. He had seen enough of Schilling on the mound to know that he had the talent to become a star in the major leagues. But he had also seen enough of Schilling in the weight room to know that Schilling didn't take his job very seriously. He joked around too much and wasn't in very good shape. Clemens thought he was squandering his talent. He had seen a number of talented players throw it all away simply because they lacked the discipline to work hard enough to get better.

That made Clemens angry. He thought that every ballplayer had a responsibility to make the most of his opportunities. After all, it provided them with a wonderful living, one that most would gladly accept. Clemens thought Schilling's attitude was disrespectful, both of the players who did work hard and of the game of baseball. Several times during his career Clemens had been injured. Each time he feared that his career was over. But each time he had come back. He treasured the opportunities to continue his career.

Across the room, Clemens watched as Schilling cracked a few jokes and lifted a few weights, what Schilling later described as "faking my way through a workout." Finally, Roger Clemens had seen enough. He asked a gym attendant to ask Schilling if he could speak to him.

The attendant went over to Schilling and said, "Roger wants to talk to you."

Schilling looked up, surprised. As he admitted to a reporter later, "I'm thinking, cool. He's one of my heroes and wants to say 'hi.'" Schilling sauntered over to the other side of the gym. Maybe, he thought, Clemens wants to teach me a new grip for my fastball. Or maybe he wants to ask me about my grip. So

Schilling smiled and said "hi," only to be greeted with a scowl. Clemens didn't want to chat or ask Schilling for advice. He wanted to chew him out.

For the next hour and fifteen minutes Roger Clemens talked and Curt Schilling listened. As Clemens remembered later, "I told him I'd talk to him about pitching if he was willing to put in the time. I told him, 'If you're not, you're gonna be just wasting your time.'" Several times he nearly cut the conversation short, wondering if Schilling was worth it or if he was even listening. As Schilling recalled later, "I can't repeat a lot of what he said . . . He just railed at me. He said I was wasting my career and I was cheating the game . . . It was one of the three or four most pivotal moments of my career . . . It was one of those conversations your father has with you when you're going down the wrong path and it saves your life."

When Clemens was done talking he sent Schilling away to think about what he had just said. He had no idea at the time if his words had any impact at all. "You can talk to somebody all you want," he said later, "but unless they take the advice and run with it, it's a waste." He left the gym shortly after.

After Clemens left, Schilling sat alone for a few moments, stung by his criticism. He wasn't angry with Clemens. He was angry with himself. He knew that Clemens was right. He *was* wasting his talent. He *wasn't* working as hard as he could. He *had* been throwing his career away.

He thought about all the energy and time he had wasted running around. In his heart he knew that he had never stepped on the pitcher's mound fully prepared. He had let down his teammates, let down himself, and let down his family.

Then Curt Schilling got up and did something he had never done before. For the next couple of hours he worked out like his career depended on it — because he finally realized it did. That night, he went to bed early, and the next day he got up and did it again. And the next day, too. His career had turned a corner. "A lot of things you learn later in life you knew all the time," he said. From that moment on, Curt Schilling took full responsibility for his life.

As Shonda said later, the talk with Clemens "came at the perfect time for Curt. It was the first time he had failed at something and didn't have his father to fall back on. He needed somebody to tell him 'This is not okay, this is what you need to do, and this is what you need to learn.' He had no father, no brothers, no uncles. Clemens filled that role."

It was time for Curt Schilling to begin the rest of his life.

Chapter Six:
1992

Starting Over

In the spring of 1992, Schilling arrived at the Astros training camp in great shape and pitched well. But as the regular season approached it became clear that Schilling really wasn't in Houston's plans anymore. Like the Red Sox and Orioles, the Astros had run out of patience waiting for Schilling to reach his potential. For an inning or two he would look like one of the best pitchers in the league. Then, inexplicably, he would give up some big hits. Or he would pitch one great game and then one bad one. Over parts of four seasons, Schilling had appeared in 100 games, winning four and losing eleven with eleven saves and 113 strikeouts in 145 innings with a 4.16 ERA. If results were all that mattered, he was just another pitcher.

The Philadelphia Phillies had a pitcher that they felt much the same way about, Jason Grimsley. Like Schilling, Grimsley had spent several seasons bouncing back and forth from the minors to the majors. He hadn't been able to fill his potential either, and the Phillies had become frustrated with him.

During the spring of 1992, the Phillies and Astros started talking and decided to swap their "potential" problems. Each thought that they could get the most out of the other's young pitcher. On April 2, 1992, Schilling was traded to the Phillies for Grimsley.

Schilling viewed the trade with mixed emotions. Houston's home ballpark, the Astrodome, was known as a "pitcher's park," a place where it was hard to score runs. That had helped Schilling. Philadelphia's home field, Veterans Stadium, didn't have the same reputation. And while he was excited that the Phillies wanted him, Philadelphia had a reputation as a tough place to play. Although Philadelphia is known as the "City of Brotherly Love," not many professional athletes agreed with that sentiment. The fans and the media were known for their high expectations for Philadelphia players. Few players had ever been able to perform well enough to satisfy them. Schilling knew they wouldn't show him much patience.

When Schilling first joined the Phillies, he was put in the bull pen. Manager Jim Fregosi and pitching coach Johnny Podres weren't very familiar with Schilling. In his first few appearances they watched him closely. They were pleasantly surprised, not only with his pitching, but by how he acted and behaved. They had heard that he was a party animal who didn't keep himself in shape or take the game very seriously. But since the conversation with Roger Clemens, Schilling had changed. He worked hard to stay physically fit and he seemed to be thinking about baseball all the time. He was constantly talking about pitching with his teammates and pestering coach Johnny Podres for ways in which he could improve.

The Phillies, who seemed to be a potential playoff team coming out of spring training, got off to a terrible start. Their starting rotation was decimated by injuries. In mid-May they decided to give Schilling a chance to start a game.

Since becoming a full-time relief pitcher with

Houston, Schilling had abandoned his full windup. As a result, his control had improved. But now that he was starting again and had to throw more pitches, both Schilling and pitching coach Johnny Podres believed he had to go back to a full windup. That way, his body could help take the strain off his arm.

Podres worked closely with Schilling to make his full windup as compact as possible so he could still retain his control. In the bull pen, it seemed to work. Schilling was anxious to try it out in a game. So on May 19 when manager Fregosi tabbed him to start against his old team, the Astros, Schilling was excited. He had always thought of himself as a starting pitcher. He was confident, but he also knew that he had to produce results. The Phillies were his fourth organization. Time was running out for him to establish himself as a front-line major league player.

On the mound, Schilling eyed the first batter, Astro second baseman and leadoff hitter Craig Biggio. Schilling felt a little odd pitching against Biggio, whom he considered a friend. But when catcher Darren Daulton flashed the signal for a fastball, Schilling put the friendship out of his head.

After years of refining his mechanics, Schilling had finally figured out how he wanted to pitch. His best pitch is what is known as a four-seam fastball, a pitch that is gripped across the seams and goes straight and fast. As he explained later, "The fastball down and away is the hardest pitch to hit. It is the point on the plate that is farthest away from the barrel of the bat and it takes the longest for the bat to get there. Every good pitcher throws away."

He knew that if he could show batters that he could throw strikes on the outside corner, they would have to look for that pitch. If they did, that meant he could also throw the ball past them on the inside, or throw a slider — a fast, short curve — even farther outside. The fastball set up everything.

That's exactly what he did to Biggio. His first pitch flashed by the outside corner for a strike. The second streaked to the inside for strike two. He then reared back and fired his best fastball. Biggio waved at the ball.

"Strike three!" yelled the umpire. The crowd at Veterans Stadium roared.

The next hitter, Steve Finley, grounded out weakly to shortstop, bringing up the Astros best batter, powerful Jeff Bagwell, one of the best fastball hitters in baseball.

But Curt Schilling was beginning to realize he was one of the best fastball pitchers in baseball. Once again, he powered fastballs to both sides of the plate before blowing the ball past Bagwell.

"Strike three!" The inning was over.

For six innings Schilling moved his fastball in and out, hitting the corners, and mixing in the occasional slider. Although he only struck out two more hitters, the Astros didn't come close to scoring. Leading 4–0 after six innings, Fregosi removed Schilling from the game. The manager knew that he hadn't pitched so many innings in one game for a long time and he didn't want Schilling to hurt his arm. The Phillies bull pen took over and preserved the lead as the Phillies won, 4–3. Curt Schilling was the winning pitcher!

As he sat in front of his locker after the game, talking to the press, he felt great. In fact, for one of the few times in his pro career, he felt as if he had been as good as he could be, that he had been prepared and pitched to the best of his ability.

Had he been younger, he probably would have

celebrated by partying long into the night. But he had grown up. He was already thinking about his workout the next day and his next start. Schilling didn't want to do anything that might affect his ability to do either. His days of irresponsibility were over.

The win earned Schilling a spot in the Phillies rotation. Each time he took the mound he seemed to pitch a little better and with even more confidence. And the more success he enjoyed, the more committed he became to continuing to do everything he could to make sure he pitched as well, if not better, the next time. Within a few short weeks it became clear that he was the best pitcher on the team and the leader of the pitching staff. Like Roger Clemens, he was learning to lead by example. When other pitchers saw how well he was pitching and how hard he was working, they began working harder too.

As the season progressed, Schilling got stronger. He pitched into the late innings almost every start, and tried to pitch a complete game whenever he could. Few pitchers tried to pitch nine innings anymore, but Schilling prided himself on his toughness and stamina. Since so many of the other Phillies starting pitchers were struggling, Schilling knew that if he pitched a complete game and saved the bull pen, they would be available to help the next Philadelphia starting pitcher. His ability to pitch complete games could help the Phillies win the next game as well.

Unfortunately, except for Schilling and Terry Mulholland, the rest of the starting staff struggled. The team was hit with a string of injuries. They fell out of the pennant race early and finished the year in last place in the National League East with a record of 70–92. But even as their season wound down, Schilling kept up his good work. He ended with a record of 14–11 with ten complete games in 26 starts and a spectacular ERA of 2.35, just behind Greg Maddux's league-leading 2.18. For the first time in his life, Schilling had spent an entire season in the major leagues.

Chapter Seven:
1993

Postseason Play

At the start of the 1993 season, few people in baseball expected Schilling to repeat his impressive performance. And who could blame them? His record at the end of 1992 seemed an anomaly compared to the ups and downs of his career. There was nothing to indicate that he was ready to become one of the best pitchers in baseball. If anything, the cards were stacked against him.

In 1992 few National League hitters knew much about Schilling's pitching. In 1993, they'd know what to expect. Many people believed that Schilling's performance would suffer. No one expected the Phillies to be very good, either. After the team finished in last place in 1992, many observers thought they would be lucky to play .500 baseball in 1993. A first-place finish or an appearance in the playoffs seemed totally

Curt Schilling rears back to deliver a lightning bolt of a pitch in a
6–1 Phillies victory in 1997.

The 1998 Cardinals don't stand a chance against the rocket arm of Phillie Curt Schilling.

Arizona Diamondback pitching greats Curt Schilling and Randy
Johnson knock knuckles as they pass each other on the field in 2001.

AP/Wide World Photos

Curt Schilling hurls a pitch in the first inning of game one of the 2001 World Series against the New York Yankees.

Curt Schilling forces out Yankee Paul O'Neill at first base in game four of the 2001 World Series.

AP/Wide World Photos

Curt Schilling is the recipient of the Roberto Clemente Award for 2001.

Randy Johnson and Curt Schilling share the 2001 World Series Most Valuable Player award.

President George W. Bush is flanked by World Series champs and MVP award winners Randy Johnson and Curt Schilling.

Curt Schilling examines his new Red Sox jersey during a news conference in 2003.

Curt Schilling pumps his fist after putting away the Yankees in the sixth inning of game six of the AL Championship.

Curt Schilling's Year-to-Year Major League Statistics

Year	Team	Wins	Losses	BB	SO	ERA
1988	Baltimore	0	3	10	4	9.82
1989	Baltimore	0	1	3	6	6.23
1990	Baltimore	1	2	19	32	2.54
1991	Houston	3	5	39	71	3.81
1992	Philadelphia	14	11	59	147	2.35
1993	Philadelphia	16	7	57	186	4.02
1994	Philadelphia	2	8	28	58	4.48
1995	Philadelphia	7	5	26	114	3.57
1996	Philadelphia	9	10	50	182	3.19
1997	Philadelphia	17	11	58	319	2.97
1998	Philadelphia	15	14	61	300	3.25
1999	Philadelphia	15	6	44	152	3.54
2000	Philadelphia	6	6	32	96	3.91
2000	Arizona	5	6	13	72	3.69
2001	Arizona	22	6	39	293	2.98
2002	Arizona	23	7	33	316	3.23
2003	Arizona	8	9	32	194	2.95
2004	Boston	21	6	35	203	3.26
Totals		184	123	638	2745	3.32

Curt Schilling's Career Highlights

1993:
Named MVP of the National League Championship Series

1995:
Winner of the Lou Gehrig Memorial Award

1997:
Member of the National League All-Star Team

1998:
Member of the National League All-Star Team

1999:
Starting pitcher of the National League All-Star Team

2001:
Winner of the World Series Championship
Named co-MVP of the World Series with teammate Randy
    Johnson
Member of the National League All-Star Team
Winner of the Players Choice Award for National League
    Most Outstanding Pitcher
Named Roberto Clemente Man of the Year

2002:
Starting pitcher of the National League All-Star Team
Winner of the Players Choice Award for National League
    Most Outstanding Pitcher

2004:
Winner of the World Series Championship

out of the question. But in 1993, both Schilling and the Phillies surprised the experts.

Schilling continued to follow a strict workout regimen in the off-season. That, plus his new attitude, paid off. On Opening Day Phillie pitcher Terry Mulholland beat the Astros. The next day Schilling notched the team's second win, with a score of 5–3. The Phillies were off and running.

The return of injured starter Tommy Greene and the addition of Danny Jackson gave the Phillies one of the best starting rotations in baseball. At the same time, players like first baseman John Kruk, third baseman Dave Hollins and outfielder Lenny Dykstra had the best seasons of their careers.

The last-place Phillies of 1992 moved into first place the first week of the 1993 season and never gave it up. Curt Schilling took the ball every fifth game and led the team with 34 starts and 235 innings while tying with Tommy Greene for the team lead with 16 wins. They won the divisional title easily.

They faced the Atlanta Braves in the National League Championship Series for the right to represent the National League in the World Series. However, despite their impressive turnaround, few people gave the Phillies a chance to beat the powerful Braves in the series.

Manager Jim Fregosi picked Curt Schilling to pitch the first game. Over the past two seasons Schilling had won over the tough Philadelphia fans with his great pitching and blue-collar approach. But to baseball fans in other parts of the country, Curt Schilling was still just a name in the box score. After all, just two years before he hadn't even been in the major leagues for a complete season. But by the end of the game baseball followers all over the country were talking about him.

Over 62,000 fans packed Veterans Stadium for game one. Everyone stood on their feet and cheered him when Schilling walked out to the mound to start the game. The cheering helped pump him up, as did the knowledge that there was one empty seat — the one he'd reserved in his father's name.

Schilling didn't care who was at bat. To remind himself to stay focused, on the bill of his cap he had written, "No talk, just get it done." He just threw the ball as hard as he could.

With his fastball topping out at 96 miles per hour, he blew away Braves leadoff hitter Otis Nixon for a strikeout. Then he struck out shortstop Jeff Blauser and finished the inning by striking out left fielder Ron Gant.

The ballpark shook as Phillies fans roared and cheered. The Phillies pushed across a run in the bottom of the first and then Schilling opened the second inning by fanning cleanup hitter Fred Mc-Griff and right fielder Dave Justice to record his fourth and fifth straight strikeouts. The streak was finally broken when Braves third baseman Terry Pendleton grounded out to end the inning.

Keyed by Schilling, the Phillies rode a wave of emotion. Even though Schilling was nicked for single runs in the third and the fourth inning, he refused to give in. Schilling pitched eight innings, striking out ten and throwing a remarkable 148 pitches before turning the game over to relief pitcher Mitch Williams. Although the Braves came back to tie the game in the ninth, costing Schilling the win, the Phillies scored a run in the tenth to win the game 4–3.

Afterward, everyone was talking about Curt Schilling's performance. And Curt was so hyped up he could hardly stop talking.

"Right now I'm tired and emotionally drained,"

he said. "I can't remember ever pitching better than that. I give a lot of credit to catcher Darren Daulton. We were pretty much in sync all night, and especially after the five strikeouts."

He credited the adrenaline rush he got from the crowd for his spectacular performance. "I've been in situations before where I've had good adrenaline early only to see it go away. You have to protect yourself from a letdown." He had done that and more.

Schilling stayed up half the night, but he wasn't out partying like crazy. He had about fifteen relatives in town for the game at his house.

Charged up by Schilling's opening game win, the Phillies surprised the Braves and beat them in six games to earn the right to play the Toronto Blue Jays in the World Series. Schilling pitched another great game in game five, reaching the ninth inning before running out of steam. Once again, although he didn't get the win, the Phillies won in extra innings. Brave Fred McGriff described Schilling's performance perfectly when he said, "He never really throws you a nice fat one. He's always inside, outside, up, down. It's really tough to zone in."

Schilling hoped the Blue Jays would soon have

the same response. But like many players, he had his good games and his bad games. In the first game of the World Series, the Blue Jays battered him for eight runs in only six innings for a Phillie loss of 8–5. They came back to win game two before dropping games three and four. If the Blue Jays won game five they would win the Series.

The Phillies turned to Curt Schilling to save the series. After game four, a 15–14 defeat that lasted more than four hours, the team was exhausted and the pitching staff worn out. Before the game, manager Jim Fregosi told Schilling that he needed him to pitch late into the game, if not complete it. Schilling nodded. He already knew.

Before the game started, catcher Darren Daulton spoke to Schilling and joked, "Just try to keep them under fourteen runs." Schilling did much better than that.

The Phillies scratched out single runs in the first two innings to take a 2–0 lead before Toronto pitcher Juan Guzman settled down. Nursing the small lead, Schilling had no margin for error. He started off strong, with pitches being clocked in the mid-90s. But by the seventh inning they were some ten miles per hour lower. When Blue Jay Paul Molitor singled with two outs that inning, Darren Daulton called time and came out to the mound.

Schilling was breathing heavily and his face was etched with fatigue. "You know you're in trouble," Daulton said to Schilling. The weary pitcher shook his head. "We'll need mirrors to get them out," added Daulton. Without a good fastball Schilling would have to try to fool the hitters.

But this was why Curt Schilling now spent so much time working out and staying in shape, so that when he was almost out of gas he'd be able to reach inside for a little more. "I looked out to the bull pen and there was nobody there," he remembered later. "I knew it was my game, and in many ways, that gave me the adrenaline to keep going."

Somehow, he got Tony Fernandez to fly out to end the inning. But in the eighth, he was in trouble again. The first two Blue Jays singled, putting runners on first and second.

All Schilling had left was his heart. His fastball was gone. All he could do was throw the ball in a good place and hope for some luck.

Rickey Henderson, one of the toughest outs in

baseball, was at bat. Henderson worked the count to 2–2 then ripped a line drive back up the middle.

Schilling had no time to react. The line drive struck him on the upper leg and careened away. "I saw Canate [the runner on third] breaking out of the corner of my eye," he said later. Schilling picked up the loose baseball and threw home. The throw was poor, but Daulton caught it and Canate stopped short of home. He was caught in a rundown and put out.

Being hit by the line drive actually helped Schilling. It gave him a jolt of adrenaline. He got the next two hitters out on sliders, striking out Devon While and getting Roberto Alomar to ground out. The Phillies still led, 2–0.

Somehow, some way, Schilling got the Jays out in the ninth inning as well. The Phillies were still in the Series. He was exhausted but ecstatic after the game. "I've always gone out with the attitude that if I didn't go nine innings I didn't do my job." There was no question that he had done his job in game five.

Unfortunately, Schilling couldn't pitch every game. In game six, the Phillies nursed a 6–5 lead into the ninth inning and were only three outs away from forcing a game seven. Then, in one of the most dramatic finishes in World Series history, Toronto outfielder Joe Carter hit a walk-off, three-run home run to win the game and the series. The Phillies had come close, but they had lost.

Schilling was disappointed, but he also knew what he and the Phillies had accomplished. Neither of them was even supposed to make it to the World Series, yet they came within two games of winning the world championship.

Now, all Schilling wanted to do was get back to the World Series.

Chapter Eight:
1994

Problems in Philadelphia

After his performance in the playoffs and World Series, Schilling seemed poised to become one of the elite pitchers of baseball. And the Phillies seemed likely to reach the postseason for the next several years.

Nothing could have been further from the truth. For just as Curt Schilling seemed to have it all figured out, everything went haywire. All the extra innings and all the tough pitches he had made in 1993 caught up with him. From the beginning of the year his arm didn't feel right and he didn't pitch as well as everyone expected. He started the season with a dismal record of 0–7. His elbow hurt and he eventually had to go on the disabled list. He didn't need to have surgery, but he did need to rest his arm. Then he hurt his knee in a freak accident and had to have surgery on that. Several other Phillies also went down with injuries. As the season progressed, the Phillies dropped further behind in the race.

It didn't matter anyway. In 1994, the players' contract with major league baseball expired and negotiations between the two sides went nowhere. On August 11 the players went on strike. Eventually, the remainder of the season was canceled. There wasn't even a World Series.

Schilling rested and tried to rehabilitate his arm, doing all sorts of special exercises. When the strike finally ended in late April of 1995, Schilling and the Phillies hoped to pick up where they had left off back in 1993.

But they couldn't. Although Schilling insisted his arm felt fine, he had lost command of his pitches during the layoff. Then in midseason of 1995 he was forced to go on the disabled list again with a sore shoulder. Minor surgery followed, sidelining him for the rest of the season. He spent the off time doing rehab, determined to be back in the lineup in 1996. His hard work paid off. After a slow start he pitched four straight complete games in September, convincing everyone he was as good as ever.

Off the field, however, changes were in the air. Schilling's existing contract with the Phillies expired at the end of the 1996 season, making him a free agent. Most Phillies fans expected him to sign with the team that offered him the most money.

But that was not the way Schilling looked at it. He liked pitching for the Phillies and wanted to stay with the team and help them reach the World Series. He and Shonda had started a family and become involved in the community. Philadelphia was home.

He knew that if the Phillies signed him to a gigantic contract, they wouldn't be able to afford to sign other quality players whose skills might give the team a chance to win the pennant. So at a time when other top pitchers were signing contracts worth ten million dollars a year, Schilling gave the Phillies what the sportswriters called a "home-town discount," signing a three-year deal worth a total of only $15.45 million, a contract he would eventually extend through 2001. When Pedro Martinez signed a contract with Boston a year later worth $12 million a season, a writer asked Schilling if he regretted signing his deal. He said he didn't. "I make more money than I'll ever need," he added.

Was this the same person who had rolled on a bed covered with twenty dollar bills only a few years earlier? Yes and no. Curt Schilling had grown as a ballplayer and, more importantly, as a person. He felt that baseball had given him so much that he owed it to the game and the fans to give something back.

He began to raise money to help fight Lou Gehrig's disease, a deadly and incurable illness that affects the body's nervous system. He even named his first son Gehrig to bring attention to the cause. He and Shonda were also heavily involved in a number of other charities. And after discovering a precancerous lesion in his mouth, Schilling also began speaking out against smokeless tobacco. He had used the product since high school even though he knew it could cause cancer. Now he was a role model for young kids and aspiring athletes. He didn't want anyone trying to imitate his bad habit, thinking it made them cool.

But Schilling still knew how to have fun. He collected baseball and war memorabilia and enjoyed showing off his collection. He retained an interest in the military passed down from his father and had always been interested in computers. He combined the two interests by playing war games on his computer. Schilling even invested in a company that makes such games and consulted with their creators.

During his time off he also realized how the computer could help his pitching. He had always kept track of how batters had performed against him. But as computer technology improved, so did Schilling's interest in using the equipment to help him become a better pitcher. Eventually, he started paying someone to record every at bat against him. Nowadays, before each start, Schilling receives a CD that shows how every hitter he is due to face has performed against him. He then uses that information to see what pitches have worked in different situations and creates a game plan for the way he intends to pitch against each hitter. Although many other big league pitchers use similar technology, few do to the same degree as Schilling. "I'm a geek," he admits.

After signing the three-year contract, Schilling rebounded in 1997 and 1998 to become one of the most dominant pitchers in baseball. During his layoff, Schilling had added muscle to his frame. This additional strength improved his stamina and gave him another mile per hour or two on his fastball. He also perfected his split-fingered fastball, which gave him another pitch to go with his slider and fastball. To throw the splitter a pitcher holds the ball deep between the index and middle finger. When thrown properly, the ball tumbles out of the hand. It looks like a fastball until just before the ball reaches home plate. Then it drops sharply.

The combination of Schilling's fastball, great control, and the new splitter gave hitters headaches. He averaged nearly ten strikeouts per start and topped 300 strikeouts in each season, the first pitcher to do so in back-to-back seasons since J.R. Richard of the Astros in 1979. Every time he pitched, fans wondered if he might set a new single game strikeout record or throw a no-hitter. He didn't, but he did pitch a number of remarkable games. One such game took place on September 1, 1997.

The world champion New York Yankees came to Philadelphia to play the Phillies in an interleague game. Fans everywhere wondered how the great Yankees would do against Curt Schilling.

It was no contest. Schilling dominated the best team in baseball, striking out sixteen Yankees in only eight innings in the 5–1 win. He struck out Derek Jeter, the Yankees star shortstop, four times. After the game a writer asked Jeter what he thought of Schilling's fastball.

"Don't ask me," Jeter answered, shaking his head. "I didn't even see it. We had no chance." Several Yankees thought Schilling was one of the best pitchers they had ever faced.

So did everyone else. When people talked about the best pitchers in baseball, a list that included the Braves' Greg Maddux, the Mariners' Randy Johnson, Roger Clemens of the Blue Jays and Pedro Martinez of the Red Sox, Schilling was also part of the discussion.

The Phillies and their fans were lucky to have him, because apart from Curt Schilling, the team wasn't very good. Even when Schilling pitched they had a hard time scoring enough runs to win. After going 17–11 in 1997, he finished in 1998 with only 15 wins versus 14 losses.

Schilling was beginning to become frustrated. He

had agreed to a modest contract because the Phillies had promised to improve the team. When they failed to do so, Schilling complained that he had been misled. The message was clear: If the Phillies didn't get better, Schilling would start to look elsewhere.

Chapter Nine:
1998–2000

Going Home?

Late in the 1998 season, Schilling noticed that his right shoulder felt loose. The more he thought about it, he realized his shoulder really hadn't felt right for more than a year. He was also puzzled because his pitches started moving differently.

As soon as the season ended he started doing his usual exercises and waited for the shoulder to improve. He was excited about the 1999 season. At long last, the Phillies had signed several pitchers to give him some help.

But in December, when he started his throwing program to prepare for the 1999 season, his shoulder still didn't feel right. He finally went to the doctor. Tests revealed that over time the muscles of Schilling's shoulder had slowly loosened. Instead of being tight and strong, his shoulder joint was loose in the front. That was causing him pain and making his pitches go awry. The doctor told Schilling there was no exercise that he could do to help the problem. He would have to have surgery.

Fortunately, the surgery could be done arthroscopically, meaning that the doctor could do the surgery through a small incision instead of a large cut. Schilling would heal in time to pitch in the upcoming season.

It was an interesting procedure. The surgeon used heat to shrink the muscles in the front of Schilling's shoulder. That tightened everything up. After he healed, the doctor not only predicted that Schilling would be good as new, he believed he would be better and probably throw even faster than before!

Still, Schilling missed about one fourth of the 1999 season. And when he did return to the lineup, it didn't matter. The Phillies were playing poorly and fell out of contention for the pennant race. In the end, the whole year was a disappointing one.

Despite this, Schilling continued to say that he wanted to stay in Philadelphia. With young stars like Bobby Abreau and Scott Rolen, he still hoped the team could turn it around. But if they didn't, he knew that there were plenty of other teams in baseball that could use one of the best pitchers in the game.

Schilling's contract included a "no-trade" clause, meaning that he couldn't be traded without his permission. In the past he had refused trade offers to teams like the Indians that had been looking for late season help. But at the start of the 2000 season he admitted that if the Phillies fell out of the pennant race, he would ask to be traded. While the Phillies were reluctant to do that, they also knew that he was a valuable player and they could trade him for some good players to help them in the future.

Early in the 2000 season, Schilling experienced more arm trouble and got off to a slow start. That just about killed the Phillies' chances for a successful season — and their chance of holding on to their star pitcher.

Still, unless Schilling's performance improved, it was possible other teams might not want him. Finally, in late June he started pitching like Curt Schilling again, winning several decisions in a row. By late July his record was 6–6. Schilling gave the club a list of the teams that he would be willing to be traded to and the Phillies started shopping him around.

At the top of the list were the Arizona Diamondbacks. They were attractive for a number of reasons, not the least of which was that Schilling would be able to return to where he grew up. But there were other reasons, too. Diamondback owner Jerry Colangelo wanted to win. In the offseason he had signed players to contracts worth more than a hundred million dollars in an attempt to buy a championship. Their pitching staff was anchored by flamethrowing Randy Johnson. Schilling was intrigued by the possibility of pitching in the same rotation with Johnson. Together, he thought they could be devastating. Since becoming a star Schilling had never been on a pitching staff with another pitcher as successful as he was.

The Phillies were looking to the future. The Diamondbacks were looking at the present. They hoped that Schilling could help them make the playoffs. The two teams started talking. If there was to be a trade, it had to be completed by the end of July. Major league baseball teams aren't allowed to make trades after August 1.

Finally, on July 26 the two teams agreed on a deal. The Diamondbacks sent pitcher Omar Daal, first baseman Travis Lee, and two minor league prospects to the Phillies in exchange for Curt Schilling. He was happy to be coming home.

Now, he not only had a chance to win, he was expected to win.

Chapter Ten:
2000–2001

A Series of Challenges

Arizona fans were ecstatic about the deal. The Diamondbacks were fighting the San Francisco Giants for the Western Division title and everyone believed that Curt Schilling would put the team over the top.

In his first appearance for the team on July 28 versus the Florida Marlins, Schilling pitched great, giving up only one run in eight innings as the Diamondbacks beat the Marlins 4–1. Arizona fans started dreaming about the postseason.

But even though the Diamondbacks had two of the best pitchers in baseball, that still wasn't enough to guarantee a pennant. They often had a hard time scoring runs and didn't have much depth. And Johnson and Schilling still had to pitch to the best of their ability.

Schilling won two of his next three starts, and the

Diamondbacks seemed poised to make a championship run over the final six weeks of the season. With several key series coming up, both Johnson and Schilling had to pitch their best. Unfortunately, Schilling was still recovering from his arm trouble and wasn't at full strength. After beating the Cubs on August 18, he won only one more game the rest of the season. The Diamondbacks slumped in September and failed to make the playoffs.

Schilling was devastated. "Ultimately I ended up being one of the reasons we didn't make the playoffs. I couldn't get it done."

He knew he had to get stronger to pitch better in 2001. As soon as the season ended he began his normal offseason routine. The Diamondbacks made a few changes, including firing manager Buck Showalter and hiring Bob Brenly. Then they showed Schilling they still had faith in his ability by signing him to a three-year contract extension. When spring training began, Schilling felt great. He was certain he was about to have his greatest season ever. Then, he suddenly realized there were more important things than baseball.

His wife Shonda had always loved being in the sun

and usually sported a deep tan. During spring training she noticed some strange spots on her body and went to the doctor. She was diagnosed with a serious case of skin cancer. Fortunately, the cancer was found before it was life-threatening. Shonda immediately underwent a series of surgeries and other treatments.

But as Schilling said later, "It made me stronger, a better husband and a better father." Just as Shonda had supported him in his struggle to overcome his addiction to smokeless tobacco after the discovery of the mouth lesion, he gave her his support. He realized that everything could change in an instant. He was determined to take advantage of every opportunity he was offered in his life.

At the start of the 2001 season, both Schilling and Randy Johnson were in their mid-thirties, an age when many pitchers start to slip. Each knew that the next pitch could be their last. But the two motivated each other. They wanted to win — now.

Their dedication was a nightmare for their opponents. Schilling generally followed Johnson in the pitching rotation. Almost every time, Johnson pitched great. Then Schilling went out and tried to pitch even better.

By midseason they were clearly the two best pitchers in baseball and among the best one–two pitching combos of all time. D-Back fans started looking ahead to the postseason. The way Johnson and Schilling were pitching, they didn't see any way they could lose.

But just as those dreams seemed about to turn into reality, everything changed. On September 11 in New York City, a group of terrorists crashed two passenger jets into the World Trade Center. More than 2,000 people were killed when the buildings collapsed. That same morning another plane flew into the Pentagon building in Washington, D.C., killing still more. A fourth planned attack never reached its intended target thanks to the heroic acts of passengers on board. Instead, the plane crash-landed in a relatively remote area of Pennsylvania. More people died in the crash, but many more could have died had the fourth attack been successful.

In the wake of the tragedies, the entire nation paused to mourn. Baseball suspended the season to give everyone a chance to recover.

Like most other Americans, the attacks deeply affected Curt Schilling, particularly the heroism shown by rescue workers, many of whom lost their lives trying to save others. Compared to what those rescuers did, playing baseball wasn't very important. Curt Schilling wanted to show his support in a meaningful way.

Before the baseball seasons resumed after a delay of more than a week, Schilling composed an open letter to "Fans of major league baseball and the victims and families" of the attacks. In the letter, he expressed the gratitude all baseball players felt toward the rescue workers and promised that they wouldn't forget what happened. "Please know," he wrote to the families of the fallen rescue workers, "that athletes in this country look to your husbands and wives as they may have looked at the men of our profession when they were young, as heroes, as idols."

The letter made it possible for Schilling to deal with his feelings and go on with the season. Like many major league players, he realized that in the wake of the attacks America needed baseball, if only to provide a few hours of relief from the sadness everyone saw on the news each day.

Somehow, Schilling and his teammates were able to refocus after the season resumed. They won the

National League West as Schilling went 22–6 for the regular season. Teammate Randy Johnson nabbed the Cy Young Award, winning 21–6, with more strikeouts and a slightly lower ERA than Schilling.

Manager Bob Brenly surprised many when he selected Schilling to pitch the opening game of the playoffs against the St. Louis Cardinals. But in recent weeks Schilling had pitched better than Johnson. Besides, in two appearances against the Cardinals in 2001, Johnson was 0–2.

Schilling made his manager look like a genius. He was almost perfect, giving up only three hits as the D-Backs won 1–0. As teammate Mark Grace said afterwards, "That was his best performance of the year. This is what he lives for." But Schilling was just getting started.

Johnson lost game two and then the two teams split the next two games. Game five, with Schilling on the mound, would determine which team would play Atlanta for the pennant.

Once again, Schilling pitched beautifully. But only four outs away from another 1–0 win, Cardinal outfielder J.D. Drew hit a home run to tie the game 1–1. But the D-Backs wouldn't be denied. In the bottom of the ninth they pushed across a run to win the game 2–1 and advance to the NLCS. "It was a hair-pulling, nail-biting experience," said Schilling.

The club looked forward to playing the Braves, who were appearing in the postseason for their tenth straight season. With a pitching staff anchored by Greg Maddux, Tom Glavine, and John Smoltz, their pitching was almost as good as Arizona's.

When Schilling took the mound for game three, the series was tied at one game apiece. Once again, he was magnificent, pitching a complete game to win 5–1. Atlanta manager Bobby Cox could only shake his head. "I thought he was on the awesome side," he said. "He's so much better than he was with the Phillies. He can spot all his pitches now." The D-Backs then swept past the Braves to win the National League pennant.

Curt Schilling was going back to the World Series.

Chapter Eleven:
2001

A Tale of Two Cities

The defending champion New York Yankees were the sentimental favorites to win the World Series. After falling behind two games to none versus Oakland in the playoffs, the Yankees came from behind to win. They then dumped the Seattle Mariners, winners of 116 regular season games, in the ALCS to make it back to the World Series. With New York still in shock over the World Trade Center attacks, most of the country found themselves rooting for the mighty Yankees, who had already won 26 world championships — more than any other team.

But in Arizona, the Diamondbacks felt differently. Although Schilling and his teammates shared everyone's anguish over the attacks, they still wanted to win the World Series. Schilling even had some fun with New York sportswriters before game one.

One asked him if he was worried about the Yankees' mystique and aura.

Schilling just laughed. "When you use words like 'mystique' and 'aura,'" he said, "those are dancers in a nightclub. These are not things we concern ourselves with on the ball field." Manager Brenly had announced that Schilling would start game one of the Series and Schilling was already telling people that if the Series went seven games, he was prepared to pitch three times.

The Series opened in Arizona where the temperature was a sweltering 94 degrees at game time. But Schilling was even hotter. He began the game throwing 97 miles per hour. He dominated the Yankees while the D-Backs roughed up New York starter Mike Mussina. After the seventh inning manager Brenly was so confident of victory he removed Schilling from the game to keep him strong. Arizona won 9–1. Although Schilling knew the Yankees were good and he respected them, he reminded everyone, "I know all about the history of the Yankees, but I wasn't pitching against [Yankee Hall of Famers] Babe Ruth and Mickey Mantle today."

In game two, Randy Johnson played "top this."

He pitched even better than Schilling and shut out the Yankees 4–0 to give Arizona a commanding 2–0 lead in the Series. Then both teams traveled to New York for game three. Soon after they arrived in the city, Schilling made sure to pay his respects at Ground Zero, the site of the World Trade Center attack. He made sure that he had the opportunity to thank some of the workers who were cleaning up the site.

The Yankees looked to be about finished, but during the postseason they had taken on the character of their city and refused to give up. In game three the Yankees turned to pitcher Roger Clemens to save them.

Curt Schilling hadn't forgotten how Clemens had turned his career around. And Clemens demonstrated that he still had a few lessons left in his strong right arm as he beat Arizona 2–1. After the game Brenly announced that Schilling would pitch game four on three days rest. He didn't want to let the Yankees back into the Series.

Game four, played under a full moon on Halloween, was an absolute classic. For the first eight innings, Curt Schilling continued his remarkable pitching. When the Diamondbacks took a 3–1 lead in the eighth inning, Brenly decided to remove him from the game and put in closer Byung-Hyun Kim. Schilling agreed with the decision. Although he told his manager he thought he could pitch another inning, he later admitted, "I was gassed. I was running on fumes."

After Kim struck out the side in the eighth, Brenly's decision looked to be the smart one. But in the ninth inning Arizona was only one strike away from victory when the Yankees rallied to tie the game. Then Derek Jeter won it with a home run in the tenth inning. The Series was tied. After the game, Brenly was heavily criticized for removing Schilling.

One day later the Yankees made another stirring comeback against Kim in the ninth inning before winning the game in the twelfth. Suddenly, the Yankees led the Series three games to two. But the Yankees didn't have the Series in the bag yet. Randy Johnson, scheduled to pitch game six, and Curt Schilling, scheduled to pitch game seven, stood in their way.

Back in Arizona for game six, the Yankees seemed to run out of steam. Arizona battered the New York pitching staff while Johnson was almost untouchable. The D-Backs crushed the Yankees 15–2 and Johnson was able to leave the game early and save his arm.

For game seven, Schilling took the mound for the third time in nine days. Knowing Schilling was already exhausted and afraid to use Byung-Hyun Kim again, Brenly took Johnson aside before the game. "Can you give me an inning tonight?" he asked the lanky pitcher. Johnson said he could. Brenly hoped the Diamondbacks would win in a blowout. But if they didn't he knew he had the two best pitchers in baseball available.

As the game started, all Schilling had left was adrenaline and fumes. He hoped that would be enough.

Pitching for New York was Roger Clemens. The opportunity to pitch against Clemens was, according to Schilling, "like the student facing the master." He had nothing but respect for his opponent. Still, he was completely confident. "If I get the ball in the seventh game," he had said before the Series, "we win."

For six innings the master and student matched

each other. Then the Diamondbacks took a 1–0 lead. If Schilling could hold on, the Diamondbacks would be champions. But in the seventh inning the Yankees knotted the score on three singles. Curt Schilling was just about out of gas.

Schilling was scheduled to come to bat in the top of the seventh. Everyone expected him to be lifted from the game for a pinch hitter. But Brenley left him in the game. One inning later, it looked as if that decision might have cost Arizona the Series.

New York's spectacular second baseman Alfonso Soriano led off the eighth inning. Schilling worked him carefully, and then threw a splitter. The pitch worked perfectly, dropping to Soriano's shoe-tops just as it approached the plate. "Unless I buried it, I couldn't have thrown it any lower," said Schilling.

But somehow Soriano got under the ball and golfed it high into the air. It came down over the fence for a home run. The D-Backs trailed, 2–1.

Too late, Brenly replaced Schilling, as first Miguel Batista, and then Randy Johnson came on in relief. But unless Arizona could score, the Yankees would be world champions. The Yankees turned the game over to their closer, Mariano Rivera. He hardly ever blew a save.

So far, the Series had been one of the most spectacular in baseball history, a World Series in which anything could happen and usually did. The bottom of the ninth inning of the seventh game was the most spectacular of all.

Schilling stayed in the dugout to watch. Mark Grace led off the inning with a soft single and was lifted for a pinch runner. Then catcher Damian Miller bunted, trying to move the runner into scoring position. He bunted the ball directly back to Rivera. The pitcher wisely threw to second to start a double play. Incredibly, his throw went wide! Both runners were safe. Arizona had a chance! Rivera looked shocked.

The end came fast. After another bunt, leadoff hitter Tony Womack doubled, tying the game. Then Luis Gonzalez came to the plate. The Yankees pulled the infield in for a play at the plate. Rivera threw. Gonzalez swung.

The pitch jammed him and broke his bat, but he still hit it relatively hard. The soft line drive floated into center field and landed safe. Jay Bell raced across home with the winning run. Curt Schilling and the Diamondbacks were world champions!

Schilling and his teammates raced onto the field and fell upon one another in a big happy pile. Schilling and Johnson appropriately shared Series MVP honors.

"We went through sports' greatest dynasty to win our first championship," said Schilling. "To beat them to win it makes it all the more special." And by pitching three times in the Series, Curt Schilling had been pretty special himself.

Chapter Twelve:
2001–2002

Pitcher Perfect

One world championship wasn't enough for Schilling. He wanted to win another. But first, it was time to celebrate. As series MVP, he was offered a trip to Disneyland. As he told his wife later, "After everything that's happened, what's more American than winning the World Series and going to Disney?"

In the offseason, the honors just kept coming Schilling's way. Major League Baseball announced that he was the recipient of the Roberto Clemente Award for his contribution to the game both on and off the field. The award, named after the Pirates star outfielder who died in a plane crash delivering relief supplies to the victims of an earthquake, meant a great deal to Schilling. Not only did it provide evidence of how dramatically he had turned his life around, but Clemente had been his father's favorite player. Schilling remembered that when Clemente passed away his father had cried. In fact, the very first major league game Schilling's father had ever taken him to was the last game Clemente played before his accident.

Then he was also named the winner of the Hutch Award named after Fred Hutchinson, a former manager who died of cancer. The award was given to a player who displays "honor, courage, and dedication while overcoming adversity in their personal or professional lives."

That was a perfect description of Schilling. Over the course of his career he had overcome his own immaturity and a series of injuries to become one of the best pitchers in the game. Then he continued to perform his best even as his wife battled cancer. And in the wake of September 11, he had taken a leadership role among baseball players in the efforts to raise funds for the families and victims, adding that to his existing charitable efforts for Lou Gehrig's disease and melanoma. It had been quite a year.

But after a brief break, Schilling resumed preparation for the 2002 season. When Randy Johnson opened the season with a shutout and Schilling also threw a shutout in his first start the next day, the two pitchers became the first defending world champs to open the season with back-to-back shutouts since 1919. Schilling hoped that would prove to be a positive omen.

Incredibly, Schilling pitched just as well in 2002 as he had in 2001, going 23–7 and striking out more than 300 hitters for the third time in his career. For a while, it looked as if he might wrest the Cy Young Award away from teammate Randy Johnson. But Schilling won only two of his last seven starts. Nevertheless, the Diamondbacks made the playoffs and looked forward to making it to the World Series again.

Unfortunately, in 2002 Schilling learned just how special the 2001 season had been. The Diamondbacks fell to the Cardinals in the first round of the playoffs. There would be no world championship for Schilling in 2002.

The 2003 season was also disappointing for the superstar pitcher, due in large part to a series of injuries. After starting only four games, Schilling was put on the disabled list for fifteen days following an appendectomy the third week of April. He returned to play on May 3, feeling fine, yet he gave up five earned runs in five innings.

But in the two weeks that followed, things started to pick up. Schilling pitched two back-to-back complete games, both shutouts, logging 24 strikeouts in 18 innings. Then, just as it seemed Schilling was getting into the zone, he was struck on the hand by a ball hit back at the mound. Initial X-rays didn't turn up any damage, but as the days went by, his hand didn't heal. A second set of X-rays was taken — and they showed the bad news. Schilling's pitching hand had broken bones. He was back on the disabled list, this time for all of June and half of July.

Schilling didn't spend his weeks off the mound relaxing. As soon as he could, he started throwing a few minutes a day until he could last as long as twenty minutes. Late in June, he made a few appearances in Triple-A games. When he returned to the Diamondbacks' mound in mid-July, fans and teammates watched anxiously to see how he would play.

That first start wasn't his best. Five runs scored in the six innings he played, and Arizona lost to the

Giants 8 to 1. But he was much stronger in his next game, against San Diego. This time he gave away only one unearned run during the seven innings he was on the mound. "I felt better," he said after the game, then added, "I still have a ways to go. There's still some things that don't feel right."

Schilling battled back against the pain in his pitching hand and by mid-August was throwing fastballs clocked at ninety-seven miles an hour. But once again, just as he was reaching peak performance, an injury got in his way. This time it was stiffness in his left knee. Examinations showed he had sustained a bone bruise. Although he didn't go on the disabled list this time, he and the Diamondback trainers kept a careful eye on the troublesome joint. Schilling's pitching, meanwhile, was less than stellar, the only highpoint being the season-high fourteen strikeouts in a game on August 23.

By early September, Schilling's knee was better, but he was being plagued with hamstring, neck, and groin pain. He finished his season on September 25 with an ERA of 2.95 and a win-loss record of 8–9. The Diamondbacks were out of the running for a playoff slot by this time. Arizona played its last game three days later, ending the 2003 season with a record of 84 wins and 78 losses.

While the rest of the world watched the best baseball teams compete to reach the World Series, Curt Schilling started to look ahead to 2004. He had one year left to go on his contract with Arizona. Schilling couldn't help but wonder how that year would go — and if it was in his best interest to stay with the Diamondbacks.

It turned out the Diamondbacks were also looking ahead to the next year. But what they were looking for was a way to trim $14 million from their budget. The fastest and most effective way to do that was to trade a big money player. Schilling, it turned out, was willing to be that player.

Rumors of a trade started to circulate. By mid-November, just weeks after the Florida Marlins had beaten the New York Yankees to become World Series champs, baseball fans knew that Curt Schilling was interested in returning to the East. The Yankees, the Phillies, and the Red Sox were on his list of possible teams he'd negotiate with. Just before

Thanksgiving, those three teams were down to one: The Boston Red Sox.

Schilling handled his own contract talks. On November 25, he and the Sox announced that they were close to a deal. Three days later, that deal was finalized. For a two-year, $25.5-million contract, Schilling agreed to waive the no-trade clause and join the Red Sox.

Boston management, fans, and team members were excited by their newest player. They had come close to their dream of making it to the World Series in 2003, only to have that dream crushed by the Yankees, their arch-rival, in the playoffs. But with the trade, their hopes surged for 2004. They already had a feared pitcher in Pedro Martinez; Schilling would be the other half of their powerful one-two punch from the mound. Perhaps that duo would even be strong enough to trounce the Yankees.

Schilling, too, seemed pleased with the trade and his future role in the ongoing battle between Boston and New York. "I like the thought of playing in the biggest rivalry in sports in front of some incredible fans," Schilling said. "The Yankee–Red Sox rivalry transcends sports. It's so much bigger than everything else in sports."

Schilling didn't have to wait long to get a taste of that rivalry. On April 17, 2004, he pitched against the Yankees for the first time. He lasted 6.1 innings, faced 28 batters, threw 121 pitches, 82 of which were strikes — and added his first win against the Yankees, his third victory of the season.

He didn't face the Yankees again until the third week of July. This time the victory went to New York. Schilling gave up ten hits in the 5.1 innings he played. It was his fifth loss of the season, bringing his win-loss record to 13 and 5.

By the time he met up with the Yankees again in late September, that record was at an astonishing 20 wins, 6 losses. The game added another to his win column — and helped vault Boston to within three and a half games of first-place New York.

Schilling didn't play the rest of the regular season, but he was the first pitcher to take the mound in the post-season. The Sox had held on to second place in the league. Now they would play against the Anaheim Angels in the Division series. The winner of that match would go on to play in the League Championships.

The star pitcher's performance wasn't stellar that game, but the Sox managed to hold on for a 9-3 win, giving them the edge in the series. During the game, Schilling had injured his ankle. At the time, he claimed the injury was minor.

The Red Sox went on to sweep the Angels in three straight games. The Yankees also beat out their opponents, the Minnesota Twins. The archrivals would face each other for the American League title and a slot in the World Series.

Schilling took the mound for the first of the seven-game series. Three innings later, he was on the bench, having pitched one of the worst games of his season. He had given up six runs in six hits; the Sox lost, 10-7.

Schilling realized his poor performance had hurt his team. He admitted later that his ankle was causing him trouble, saying that if it didn't get better, he wouldn't play again. Instead, he watched with growing dismay as his team dropped two more games, including a 19-8 pasting in game three. The Sox were in the hole, three games to none.

Baseball fans everywhere knew the Sox were unlikely to turn this series around. After all, no team ever in the history of Major League Baseball had come from a 3-0 deficit to win the pennant.

But the Sox weren't beat yet. Game four, played in Boston, went an exhausting twelve innings. The match ended with a victory for the Red Sox, thanks to an amazing effort by slugger David Ortiz, who batted in two runs in the bottom of the fifth inning, then belted in the game-winning homer in the twelfth.

Game five went even longer — fourteen innings! Again, Ortiz proved the hero, slamming in the last homer of the night to give the Sox a 5-4 victory.

Curt Schilling returned to the mound for game six. He threw ninety-nine pitches in seven innings and gave up just one run. It wasn't until midway through the game that the cameras picked up what many had missed. Blood was seeping through one of Schilling's socks.

Fans found out later that Schilling had undergone minor surgery to his injured ankle that morning so he could play that night. The pain had to have been awful, but Schilling didn't let it bother him. He just played the best he could. And that best was just what the Sox needed. They left the stadium with another win to tie up the series at three games apiece. Game seven would decide if the Sox or the Yankees were in the World Series.

Nine innings later, the Red Sox made history. They beat the Yankees 10-3 in what Red Sox owner John Henry called, "The greatest comeback in baseball history." Boston was going to the World Series.

After the amazing turnaround in the playoffs, the World Series held little drama. The Sox beat the St. Louis Cardinals in four straight games. Schilling, his injured ankle still raw from surgery, pitched six innings of the second game victory to bring his 2004 season record to 22 wins, 7 losses, the best of any pitcher in the MLB.

Schilling's ankle was operated on in early December and now the star pitcher is looking forward to the 2005 season. No one who plays with or against him doubts that he will be a force to be reckoned with for years to come. For he is a player, and a person, who has continued to beat the odds and accomplish what has often seemed impossible. Even more important, he has grown as a human being and learned to make a difference in people's lives.

"That," says Curt Schilling, "is pretty much the basis of why we're put on Earth, I think."

Matt Christopher®

Sports Bio Bookshelf

Lance Armstrong

Kobe Bryant

Jennifer Capriati

Terrell Davis

Julie Foudy

Jeff Gordon

Wayne Gretzky

Ken Griffey Jr.

Mia Hamm

Tony Hawk

Grant Hill

Ichiro

Derek Jeter

Randy Johnson

Michael Jordan

Mario Lemieux

Tara Lipinski

Mark McGwire

Greg Maddux

Hakeem Olajuwon

Shaquille O'Neal

Alex Rodriguez

Curt Schilling

Briana Scurry

Sammy Sosa

Venus and
Serena Williams

Tiger Woods

Steve Young

Read them all!

*Originally published as *Crackerjack Halfback*

All available in paperback from Little, Brown and Company